AMAZING ANIMALS

WARTHOGS

BY ASHLEY GISH

CREATIVE EDUCATION • CREATIVE PAPERBACKS

Published by Creative Education
and Creative Paperbacks
P.O. Box 227, Mankato, Minnesota 56002
Creative Education and Creative Paperbacks
are imprints of The Creative Company
www.thecreativecompany.us

Design by The Design Lab
Art Direction by Graham Morgan
Production by Blue Design

Images by Getty Images/Londolozi Images/Mint Images, 6, Martin Harvey, 21, McDonald Wildlife Photography Inc., 5, Staffan Widstrand, 18; Pexels/Dario Fernandez Ruz, 2, Filip Olsok, 14, Frans van Heerden, 15, Magda Ehlers, 8, S K, 13, SK Movies & Photos, 7; Wikimedia Commons/Biodiversity Heritage Library, 23, Charles J. Sharp, cover, 1, 9, 10, 17, Diego Delso, 2, 3, 4, 5, 6, 7, 8, 10, 11, 12, 13, 14, 15, 16, 18, 19, 20, 22, 24, Pearson Scott Foresman, 16

Cataloging-in-Publication data is available from
the Library of Congress.
Library Binding ISBN: 9798895810613
Paperback ISBN: 9798896800149
eBook ISBN: 9798895811870
LCCN: 2025011194

Printed in China

Table of Contents

The "warts" on warthogs' faces are thick patches of skin.

Warthogs are fierce-looking wild pigs that live in **sub-Saharan Africa**. They are named for the wart-like bumps on their skin. These hogs may look tough, but they usually run away from danger with their tails held high.

sub-Saharan Africa all parts of Africa south of the Sahara desert

Even though they do not usually live together, warthogs peacefully share resting, feeding, and drinking areas.

Warthogs are important grassland animals. They turn the soil when they look for food. This helps plants grow. Warthogs also provide a food source for large **predators** like lions and leopards.

predator an animal that hunts other animals for food

A warthog's spiral-shaped upper **tusks** *can be up to two feet (60 centimeters) long!*

Warthogs have coarse hairs all over. A bristly mane runs from their head to their rump. Their large tusks are used for digging and fighting. The bumps on their faces protect them when they fight with each other.

tusk a long tooth that sticks out of the mouth

There are two kinds of warthogs. Common warthogs are heavy and live in grass- and woodlands. Desert warthogs are slimmer, with longer legs than common warthogs. They live in the deserts of Somalia, Ethiopia, and Kenya.

Warthogs can go months without water during dry seasons.

Warthogs may dig up and eat farm crops. Farmers may kill warthogs that steal food this way.

Warthogs are omnivores. They eat things like grass, seeds, fruit, and leaves. They dig through the dirt to find nuts and roots. They may sometimes eat the meat of dead animals they find.

omnivore an animal that eats plants and meat

Male warthogs are called boars. Females are called sows. Boars and sows come together to mate. Sows give birth after about six months. Piglets and their mothers may live in groups called sounders. Up to 40 sows and piglets may live in a sounder.

A mother warthog usually has two or three piglets, though she can have up to eight.

Boars fight each other to mate with sows during mating season. They use their lower tusks as weapons. They squeal and grunt loudly when they fight. The losing boar runs away with his tail in the air.

Warthogs can run up to 34 miles (55 kilometers) per hour. That's about as fast as a racehorse!

Warthogs may not be pretty, but they are smart. If people try hunting them during the day, warthogs hide and come out at night instead. Birds use special calls when predators are near. Warthogs recognize the calls and run away!

Oxpeckers are small birds that perch on warthogs and pick off ticks, acting like a cleaning service.

Warthogs do not have fur to keep them warm at night. They sometimes line their **burrows** *with grass for added warmth.*

Warthogs live in burrows left empty by aardvarks. They sleep, raise their piglets, and hide from predators inside their burrows. Burrows keep warthogs cool during the day and warm at night.

burrow a hole in the ground where some animals live

A Warthog Tale

Long ago,

Warthog was handsome. But he was a bully. After making fun of Lion, Warthog ran to his burrow. He did not know Porcupine was napping inside. Warthog got a face full of Porcupine's quills. They made Warthog's face lumpy and scarred forever.

Read More

Joubert, Beverly. *The Ultimate Book of African Animals*. Washington, D.C.: National Geographic Kids, 2021.

Levy, Janey. *Warthogs and Mongooses*. New York: Gareth Stevens, 2021.

Websites

Warthog
https://kids.nationalgeographic.com/animals/mammals/facts/warthog
See more pictures and learn more about warthogs on National Geographic Kids.

Warthog
https://sdzwildlifeexplorers.org/animals/warthog
Read more about warthogs on the San Diego Zoo Wildlife Explorers website.

Index